Great
BUILDING
Stories of the Past

Great
BUILDING
Stories of the Past

Peter Kent

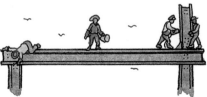

OXFORD
UNIVERSITY PRESS

OXFORD
UNIVERSITY PRESS

Great Clarendon Street, Oxford OX2 6DP

Oxford University Press is a department of the University of Oxford.
It furthers the University's objective of excellence in research, scholarship,
and education by publishing worldwide in

Oxford New York

Athens Auckland Bangkok Bogotá Buenos Aires
Cape Town Chennai Dar es Salaam Delhi Florence Hong Kong Istanbul
Karachi Kolkata Kuala Lumpur Madrid Melbourne Mexico City Mumbai
Nairobi Paris São Paulo Shanghai Singapore Taipei Tokyo Toronto Warsaw

with associated companies in Berlin Ibadan

Oxford is a registered trade mark of Oxford University Press
in the UK and in certain other countries

British Library Cataloguing in Publication Data available

Hardback ISBN 0-19-910783-1
Paperback ISBN 0-19-910784 X

1 3 5 7 9 10 8 6 4 2

Printed in Italy

CONTENTS

INTRODUCTION

Our modern civilisation rests on the work of architects and engineers. The buildings we live and work in, the roads and railways we travel on, even, in some places, the ground we stand on, are all the work of architects and engineers. A civilisation is in its buildings.

A termite mound.

The first people in the world were nomads who moved around in search of food. The first structures they built were probably simple shelters made of branches. In those prehistoric times, animals were greater engineers than people. Ants and termites built huge skyscraper mounds, wasps and birds made complicated nests, burrowing animals excavated tunnels and beavers dammed

A beaver's dam.

rivers. Animals then, as now, had the three things necessary for successful engineering. The first is skill – all rabbits, for instance, know how to dig, it is part of their nature. The second is equipment – beavers, for example, have front teeth adapted for cutting through wood. The third is organisation. Ants by instinct obey the rules of ant society and work together. Although each individual ant is small, millions of them working to a common purpose can build something very large.

Early humans had virtually no tools, few skills, and not much organisation. However, they did have one great asset – they had intelligence and the ability to learn. They were ingenious – from which we get our word 'engineer'. It is quite possible that people learnt the basics of engineering from observing animals. Over time, as people learnt how to grow food, instead of having to wander about to find it, stable communities were established and civilisation began to develop. By then there was a larger labour force that could work together on building projects.

An Assyrian official organising diggers.

A hill fort.

Probably the first large-scale civil engineering projects were in digging irrigation ditches and raising earth banks to control the flow of rivers, to benefit agriculture. Other large-scale projects would have been building defences. In the Middle East these were mud brick or rough stone walls, in Western Europe they were ditches beside wooden fences and towers. The size of these forts is still impressive today. Religion was another powerful inspiration to build. All over the world people raised mounds, towers and constructions of wood and stone to act as temples or tombs.

The ancient monument of Stonehenge.

Before construction could really take off, people had to develop basic tools, and an understanding of how to use simple machines such as levers and rollers. They also had to learn how to count and measure, so they could make designs and plans. Around the world, people built using their local materials. In some places wonderful bridges and buildings were built out of nothing more than bamboo and woven grass, in other places everything was made from mud, and in others it was wood. Whatever the material, however, the principles behind the structure, the basic rules that made it stand up, were the same.

An early idea for bridge building.

Building has made wonderful advances in the last 5000 years, as the following pages celebrate. But the greatest step was taken right at the beginning. That was when people learnt that if they worked together, if they used their ingenuity, with simple tools, patience and hard work they could change the world – and they did.

GREAT PYRAMID

The Great Pyramid at Giza, in Egypt, is the oldest and largest surviving stone structure built by humans. This stupendous piece of engineering amazed the ancient Greeks, who were the first tourists to visit it, and it continues to fascinate and impress millions of visitors today. Five thousand years after it was built, it is still doing its job of celebrating the power and fame of the pharaoh Khufu.

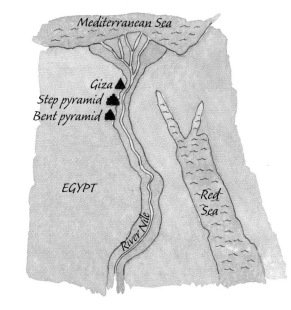

Imhotep was a high priest of the sun-god, Re. He is the first architect whose name we know. After he died he was worshipped as a god.

Between about 2600 and 1640 BC more than 80 pyramids were built along the banks of the River Nile in Egypt. They were intended to be tombs for the pharaohs, or rulers. The first was designed by a priest called Imhotep, for pharaoh Djoser. This pyramid rose in six steps, but from then on pyramids were built with smooth sides. In about 2500 BC the Great Pyramid for Khufu was built.

The pharaoh of Egypt was more than just a king. He was regarded as a living god, and was all-powerful. He spoke directly to the gods in the temples, he ran the government and led his country in war. Such a powerful figure needed an impressive tomb, one that would keep his body safe for ever. And Khufu's tomb is certainly impressive. It stands 146 metres high, made with 2.3 million blocks of limestone. Amazingly, considering the tools the Egyptians had, it took only about 23 years to build and was ready just in time to receive the body of the pharaoh.

A cross section of Imhotep's step pyramid. It began as a raised platform, was extended to have four steps, and was later enlarged to have six.

first pyramid

original tomb

underground burial chambers

61 metres

The peculiar bent pyramid of King Sneferu. The sides change from an angle of 54⁰ to 43⁰, probably because the builders realised the first angle was too steep.

burial chambers

105 metres

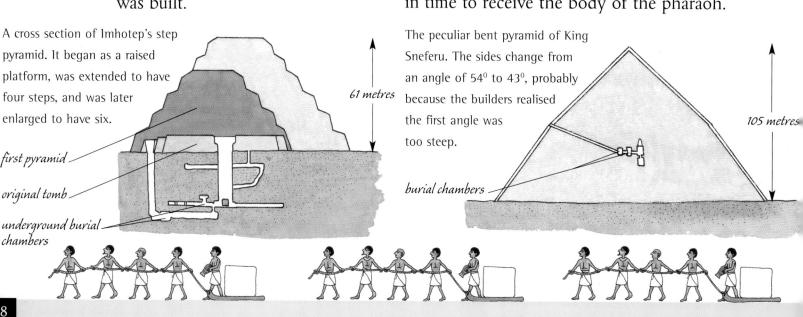

The shape of a step pyramid was meant to represent the steps the pharaoh would climb to the stars.

The change to the smooth-sided pyramid is thought to represent the belief that, after his death, the pharaoh would climb the rays of the sun to the sun god Re.

The pyramid is actually a very simple building, a solid pile of stone with a small burial chamber for the pharaoh deep inside. It was built by teams of workers, who were free men not slaves. There was a full-time work force of skilled craftsmen, and they were helped for three months of the year by peasants unable to work because the Nile had flooded their fields. They lived in specially built villages around the site, and were paid in food and lodging. The technology they used was very simple. Their tools were made of soft copper, not iron, and as the wheel had not yet been invented they dragged the massive stone blocks on sledges, using wooden rollers and levers to position them.

Surveyors checked that each side was the same length, and that the slope was a constant 52°. The outer layer of stones was cut to shape and polished once they were in place.

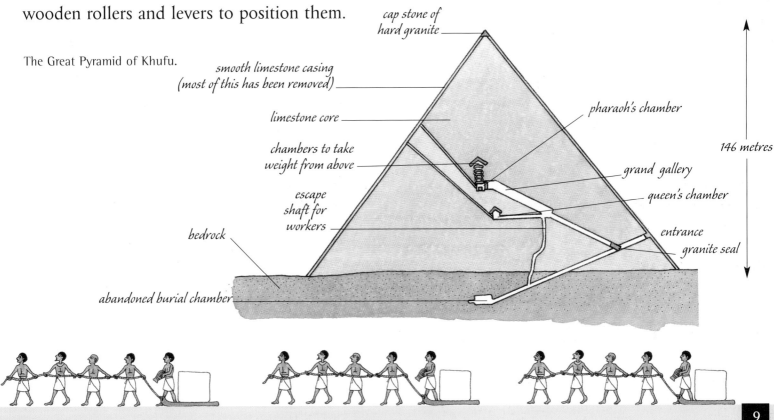

The Great Pyramid of Khufu.

cap stone of hard granite

smooth limestone casing (most of this has been removed)

limestone core

chambers to take weight from above

escape shaft for workers

bedrock

abandoned burial chamber

pharaoh's chamber

grand gallery

queen's chamber

entrance granite seal

146 metres

Although the Great Pyramid remains a wonderful monument to Khufu, it failed to protect his body and all the rich goods in his tomb. When archaeologists first examined the inside of the pyramid about 150 years ago, they found it completely empty. Everything had been taken by tomb robbers thousands of years before. The pharaohs carried on building pyramids for another thousand years, but they never built another as big as Khufu's.

The Egyptians' success in building came from their efficient organisation. This would not have been possible without scribes to draw up plans and keep records.

The measurements of Egyptian buildings are very accurate. Egyptian surveyors used simple instruments, but were very skilled.

Most of the pyramid is made from limestone blocks quarried nearby. The outer casing was made of better quality stone from Tura across the Nile. Each block weighs about $2\frac{1}{2}$ tonnes. They are set in a thin layer of lime mortar. When the pyramid was complete, with a smooth, polished white skin, it must have been a dazzling sight.

This ramp would have needed a vast amount of material.

This ramp used less material.

This ramp would have been very steep.

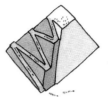

It would have been difficult to turn the corners on this ramp

This ramp covered the edges, which surveyors would have needed to see.

This ramp is the latest to be suggested.

The stones were raised by a ramp. No one is quite sure how this was arranged, but there have been many theories.

About 20,000 workers probably built the Great Pyramid.

The Egyptians in 2500 BC had not invented the wheel. The stones were dragged on wooden sledges along roadways made of timber and packed clay.

GREAT WALL OF CHINA

The Great Wall stretches over 5000 km across China. Its twisting course has often been compared to the body of a dragon.

The largest and longest construction project in history is the Great Wall of China. Millions of peasants and soldiers worked over a period of 1800 years to build the most formidable frontier defence in the world. The Great Wall runs for over 5000 kilometres, from the Gobi Desert in the west to the sea in the east, through some spectacular mountainous country.

Emperor Shihuangdi. He is also remembered by the extraordinary collection of 7000 lifesize terracotta soldiers that guard his tomb.

Defensive walls were first built in northern China before 3000 BC, but the main work of building the Great Wall was begun in the reign of the first emperor, Shihuangdi of the Qin dynasty. He united the various Chinese kingdoms under his rule in 221 BC. He sent a huge army of 300,000 soldiers, commanded by General Meng Tian, to defeat the nomad peoples to the north of the empire and to build a defensive wall to keep them out. This wall was made of layers of earth, stones and twigs rammed hard inside a wooden frame.

Very little of it has survived, for it was added to and rebuilt over the next thousand years. In AD 446 the emperor Taiping Zhenjun sent 300,000 men to build another section, and a hundred years after that 1.8 million peasants were forced to build a stretch over 120 kilometres long. The Tang dynasty emperors (618-907) then neglected the wall.

The Chinese invented the wheelbarrow.

Bricks and stones were carried in panniers by donkeys.

An ingenious invention was an endless chain of baskets, like a modern dredger.

Most of the early wall was built of rammed earth. Layers of earth up to 10 cm thick were separated by mats of reeds and twigs, then pounded by hard wooden mallets.

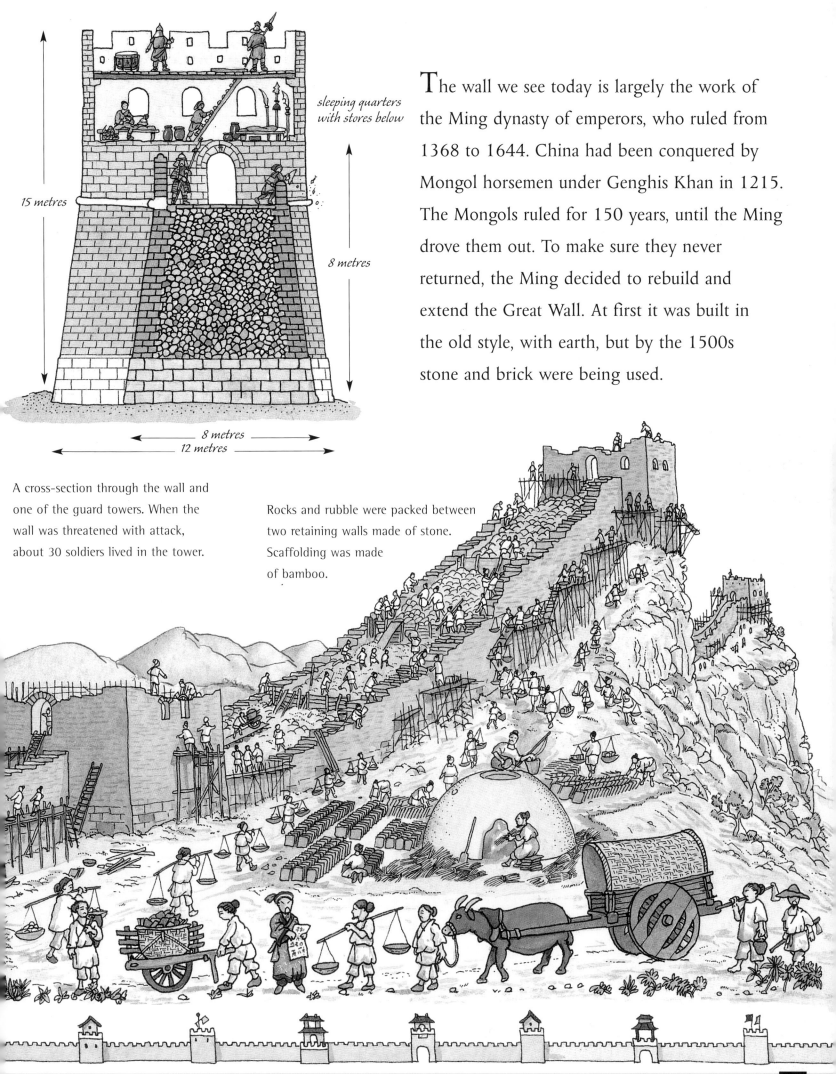

15 metres

sleeping quarters
with stores below

8 metres

8 metres

12 metres

The wall we see today is largely the work of the Ming dynasty of emperors, who ruled from 1368 to 1644. China had been conquered by Mongol horsemen under Genghis Khan in 1215. The Mongols ruled for 150 years, until the Ming drove them out. To make sure they never returned, the Ming decided to rebuild and extend the Great Wall. At first it was built in the old style, with earth, but by the 1500s stone and brick were being used.

A cross-section through the wall and one of the guard towers. When the wall was threatened with attack, about 30 soldiers lived in the tower.

Rocks and rubble were packed between two retaining walls made of stone. Scaffolding was made of bamboo.

The Great Wall was not just a wall, but a very complex system of frontier defences. Along parts of it there were towers every 200 metres and hundreds of forts and castles. A system of beacons could send warning messages along the wall, and call up reinforcements from the forts and barracks behind. Every gateway was elaborately defended, and in many places there were three or more lines of defence. The wall was cleverly sited on mountain ridges and hills, so that it always occupied higher ground than the enemy. It is this feature that makes it look so spectacular as it winds its way across the country. It also made it incredibly difficult to build. All the materials had to be dragged up steep slopes and narrow mountain paths. At its most impressive, to the north of the city of Beijing, the wall was over 7.5 metres high and 9 metres wide.

At times over a million soldiers defended the wall. They also farmed the land nearby, to feed themselves. By the 1800s the wall was no longer maintained as a serious defence. It last saw action in the 1930s, when the Japanese invaded, but now the only danger it faces is the tramping feet of millions of tourists.

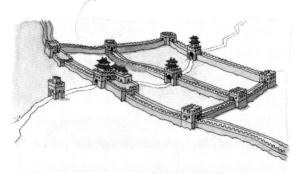

Places where the enemy were most likely to attack were made extra strong. This complicated triple gate defended the important Xifengkou Pass.

Nomad horsemen without proper seige equipment found it difficult to break through the wall if the defending troops were ready and organised. The Chinese had invented gunpowder in about AD 800, but used it in military fireworks, not cannons. Early rockets and grenades made a lot of smoke and noise, but were not very dangerous.

東

guard tower

gate

barracks

beacon tower

fort

直星

This map of a section of the Great Wall shows that it was not just a simple line of wall, but a complicated defence system.

Beauvais Cathedral

Eight hundred years ago Europe was in the grip of a frenzy for building cathedrals, churches of such size and magnificence they would glorify God and show off the people's pride in their building skills and their city.

One master mason, Hugues Libergier, was famous enough to have a tomb in Reims cathedral.

This carved ox stands on the tower of Laon cathedral. There is a legend that it miraculously helped build the cathedral by hauling stone without needing to be led.

Starting in France, but soon spreading far and wide, cities competed to raise some of the tallest and most daring structures in stone that the world had ever seen. Each new cathedral was built higher than the last, as if trying to reach heaven itself. The rich gave their money and the poor gave their labour on the building sites. At Chartres in France people were so eager to see the work finished, they harnessed themselves to carts and dragged stones from the nearby quarry.

The old cathedrals had a barrel vault, that needed support along a continuous edge. Walls were thick and windows were small.

In the new Gothic style, the downward forces of the vault are concentrated in four points. The walls can be opened up.

Vaulted roofs made of ribs in a pointed arch were stronger and lighter than the old style.

Old style rounded windows

The stone frames, or tracery, in the new windows was carved into elaborate patterns.

wooden roof

stone vault

boss

rib

flying buttresses supported the enormously high roof.

aisle

nave

column

(red lines indicate lines of force)

This stained glass window from Beauvais shows the master mason checking the level of a course of stones.

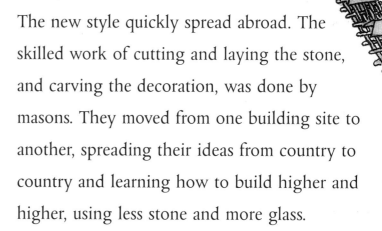

Medieval builders designed many ingenious machines to help in their work, like this crane. Two men turned the treadwheel to wind the rope.

Until that time, cathedrals had been built in a style copied from the ancient Romans. They were low and dark with thick walls, and the arches over the windows and doors were semicircular. In 1140 the first church to be fully constructed in a new style of architecture, called Gothic, was built at St Denis, near Paris. It was a sensation: no-one had ever seen anything like it. It was tall and filled with light that streamed in through huge windows of coloured glass.

The new style quickly spread abroad. The skilled work of cutting and laying the stone, and carving the decoration, was done by masons. They moved from one building site to another, spreading their ideas from country to country and learning how to build higher and higher, using less stone and more glass.

Gargoyles were stone spouts to shoot rainwater clear of the walls. They were often carved in the shape of monsters.

Hundreds of statues decorated the cathedrals inside and outside. This angel is from Reims.

The inside walls were covered with brightly painted pictures, telling stories from the Bible.

At last the limits were reached, at Beauvais in France. Here the nave was 48 metres high – so tall a 16-storey building could fit inside. The tower, 150 metres high, was probably the tallest structure in the world at that time. This was the very limit of the stone masons' skill – and something went wrong. Either the foundations or the buttresses were not strong enough, and the nave collapsed. A century later, the vast tower fell too. The cathedral we see at Beauvais today is only part of the original that must have towered above the small city like a mountain, but still it is a spectacular monument to the faith and skill of those medieval master builders.

The pinnacles on the flying buttresses added extra weight as well as decoration.

The stone ribs of the vaults were built on a temporary wooden framework.

The stone vaults were covered by a steep wooden roof, covered with slates.

Straw protected unfinished walls from damage caused by frost.

Eddystone Lighthouse

Ever since people first built boats, we have faced the dangers of the sea. Great ocean waves are dangerous, but rocks and sandbanks close to the shore are even more deadly, and over the centuries have sunk thousands of ships. This is the amazing story of how men overcame one of the greatest building challenges – how to build at sea.

The Pharos, at Alexandria in Egypt, was one of the seven wonders of the ancient world. It was 140 m high, and stood for over 1500 years.

Sailors usually drowned when their ships were wrecked, partly because there were few lifeboats but also because most of them could not swim.

By 1700 many lighthouses had been built along coasts and in harbours, such as the Lanterna at Genoa in Italy, or La Tour de Courdouan at the mouth of the River Gironde in France, but the problem remained of how to warn sailors of the dangers out at sea. Bells fixed on to rocks worked for a while, before they were washed away, but only in daylight. Off the south coast of England, near Plymouth, the Eddystone Rock had claimed hundreds of ships over the centuries. More and more ships were sailing through this area at the end of the 18th century, as trade increased between England and America, so the need to light Eddystone Rock was becoming ever more urgent.

One man, called Henry Winstanley, decided he would find a solution. He was not an engineer, but an artist. Still he decided to build a tower out on the rock, where a lighthouse keeper could live to make sure the bright lamp at the top was always lit. He began work in 1696. It was a slow process, as work could only be done at low tide, but within two years his lighthouse was finished. In 1698 light blazed out from Eddystone Rock for the first time. It was a momentous day.

wind vane

ornamental candlesticks

lantern lit by
38 tallow candles

crane

Winstanley strengthened his tower over the
following year, but one night, in November
1703, the greatest storm that England has
ever known smashed his creation to pieces.
Winstanley, who was spending the night
on the tower, disappeared with it.

The following day a ship hit the rock
and sank with all on board.

chute to drop stones
on an enemy

Winstanley's tower was 24 m high
and made mainly of wood. The
bottom part was stone, and was
fixed to the rock by iron rods.

A replacement lighthouse
was built in 1709 by
another amateur, John
Rudyerd. Again it was
made of wood, and in
1755 the candles in the
lantern caused a fire that
destroyed it.

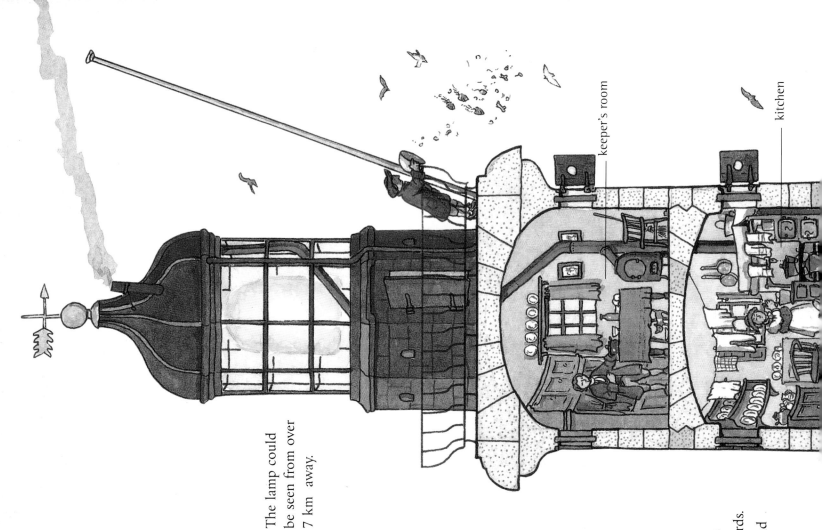

The lamp could
be seen from over
7 km away.

keeper's room

kitchen

Smeaton based the shape
of his tower on an oak
tree — thick at the bottom
and gently tapering upwards.
It weighed 988 tonnes and
cost £16,000 to build.

John Smeaton was born in 1724
and developed civil engineering
into an exact science. As well as
designing cranes and diving
equipment, he built harbours
and bridges. He died in 1792,
worn out, it was said, by
all his hard work.

A new solution to the problem had to be found,
and soon. The new designer was John Smeaton, an
engineer who was used to the problems of building
at sea. He first studied the power of waves in a
scientific manner, and realised that the lighthouse
must be built of hard stone, to withstand the
pounding of the waves. He chose granite.
His most brilliant idea was to make all the stones
interlock with each other, and bind them with
a special cement, devised by him, that would
not be worn down by water.

store room

After three long years, Smeaton's Tower was finished.

The lamp, holding 24 candles, was lit for the first time in 1759.

For over 120 years this amazing structure withstood the fiercest

storms – and saved the lives of thousands of sailors. In the end,

it was the rock, rather than the lighthouse, which crumbled first.

In 1882 Smeaton's Tower was carefully taken down, and rebuilt

at Plymouth where it stands today. A new lighthouse was built

beside it, where it remains a welcome sight for sailors

passing the treacherous Eddystone Rock.

All the stones were first
assembled on dry land at
Plymouth to make sure
they fitted exactly.

The stones were carefully cut
into the Eddystone Rock to
make a completely solid base.

The cement was made of
quicklime clay, sand and
crushed iron slag.

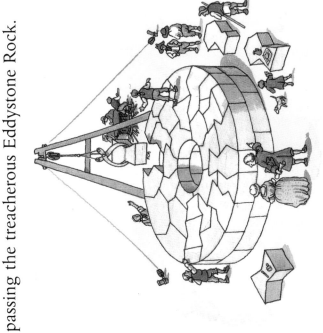

BROOKLYN BRIDGE

John A. Roebling

Emily Roebling

Washington A. Roebling

New York, the greatest city and harbour in the United States, is really a collection of separate cities ringing the huge harbour of New York Bay. The most famous part, with all the skyscrapers, is Manhattan Island, with the waters of the Hudson River on one side and the East River on the other.

Until the middle of the 19th century the only bridges to Manhattan were across the narrow channel at the north end of the island. Ferry boats were the only way to cross the wide Hudson and East Rivers. The confusion and danger were great, as ferries darted through the lines of sea-going ships that went up and down the rivers. In winter, ice blocks filled the rivers and all river traffic stopped.

The solution was obvious – a bridge – but it would be very difficult to build one. The rivers were wide and deep, and would have to be crossed with a single span. A conventional bridge, with arches, would not do. It would have to be a suspension bridge, high enough above the water to allow sailing ships with tall masts to pass beneath.

In 1867 it was finally decided to build a bridge between Manhattan and Brooklyn. John A. Roebling was chosen to design it. He had become famous for building a suspension bridge across the Niagara Falls, a gigantic waterfall in Canada. Roebling planned a bridge with a huge span of 486 metres. It would be the longest suspension bridge in the world.

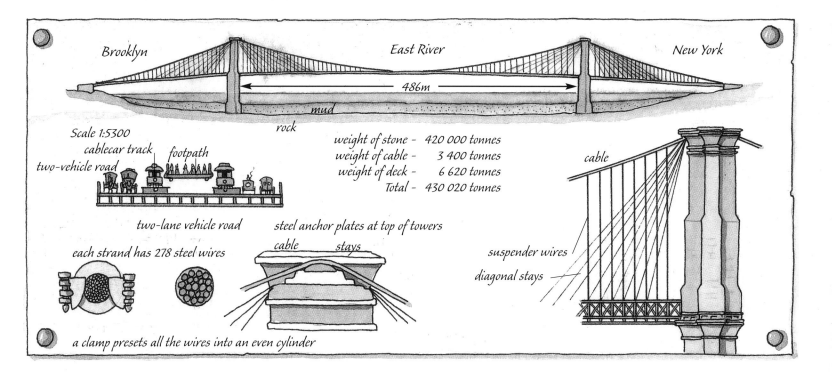

Brooklyn   East River   New York

486m

mud

rock

Scale 1:5300

cablecar track   footpath

two-vehicle road

weight of stone -   420 000 tonnes
weight of cable -   3 400 tonnes
weight of deck -   6 620 tonnes
Total -   430 020 tonnes

cable

two-lane vehicle road

steel anchor plates at top of towers

cable   stays

suspender wires

diagonal stays

each strand has 278 steel wires

a clamp presets all the wires into an even cylinder

Tragically, John A. Roebling never saw work begin on his bridge. Down at the docks one day his foot was crushed by a ferry boat, and he later died of tetanus. His son, Washington A. Roebling, took over as chief engineer and started work.

When the caissons reached the rock they were filled with concrete. They had to be filled with compressed air at high pressure to stop the water flooding in. This was very dangerous. The towers were then built on top of them.

The first job was to build the foundations for the two huge towers. The riverbed where these had to stand was sand and slimy mud, with solid rock over 30 metres below. Roebling designed two giant cylinders, called caissons, that would gradually sink down as the workmen dug out the sand and mud. Roebling was injured as these were built, but he carried on directing work from his sickbed. His wife, Emily, learned engineering so she could supervise work on the site.

Roebling moved to a house from where he could see the bridge slowly going up.

Once the towers were finished, it was time to string between them the huge cables from which would hang the roadway below. These cables were the Roeblings' great invention. Up until then, cables of suspension bridges had been made either of chains or of several wire ropes twisted together, hauled up to span the gap between the towers. The cables for Brooklyn Bridge would have been far too long and heavy to do this. The Roeblings had the idea of making them of hundreds of steel wires running side by side, bound together by wire to form one huge, strong cable. The main advantage of this was that it could be strung one strand at a time, by a grooved spinning wheel passing back and forth between the towers.

The most difficult job was getting the first wire in position. It was laid from the tower tops and under the water. Early one Sunday morning in 1876 the wire was hoisted into the air. A single wire now joined Manhattan and Brooklyn. The

spinning wheels buzzed back and forth between the towers like a mechanical spider, spinning over 10,000 steel wires. These were then all squeezed together and bound with wire.

When the cables were fixed, it was time to make the roadway. Washington A. Roebling was still ill, but Emily carried on the work until finally, in 1883, the bridge was finished. It had cost $15 million and over 20 lives.

Americans were very proud of their new bridge. They thought it was one of the wonders of the world, and rightly so for the basic methods used in building it have never been bettered. It still carries a torrent of traffic above the East River. Every other suspension bridge in the world is a descendant of the mighty Brooklyn Bridge, and owes much to the three brave and ingenious Roeblings.

The honour of being the first person to cross the Brooklyn Bridge was given to Emily Roebling. As she crossed, bands played, cannons fired from forts in the harbour, ships hooted and vast crowds cheered.

EIFFEL TOWER

Throughout history, and all over the world, people have raised towers, from simple earth mounds to intricate, stone spires. The challenge was always to raise these higher and higher. In the 19th century, developments in the technology of using iron in building meant that structures could reach dizzying heights never previously imagined.

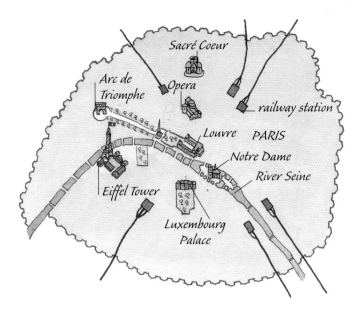

In 1884 the French government announced that there would be an international exhibition in Paris, opening in 1889, to celebrate the 100th anniversary of the French Revolution. The main attraction would be a tower, 300 metres high. They held a competition to find the best design, and out of more than 100 entries they chose the plans of Alexandre Gustave Eiffel. Eiffel was the most famous and successful engineer in France. He had designed and built more than 40 large railway bridges, many buildings and the frame that supported the giant Statue of Liberty in New York.

He had perfected a method of making strong but light structures from wrought iron. Not one of his bridges collapsed, which was an unusual record for an engineer at that time. By the time the government had chosen his design, the opening of the exhibition was less than two years away. Eiffel and his team had to work fast. Eiffel and his designers planned the tower with absolute precision. First every detail was drawn on a separate plan, in over 5000 drawings. The complete order of assembly was carefully worked out, so that when work began the tower could be fitted together quickly.

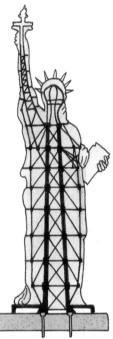

The skin of the Statue of Liberty, New York, is made of thin copper sheets, which would not stand up without the support of Eiffel's wrought iron skeleton.

Just imagine these in the place of the Eiffel Tower! Four of the rejected designs from the competition.

The tower was made of iron girders, joined together by rivets. All the girders were made in Eiffel's factory, where they were joined into pieces not more than 5 metres long. These pieces were then assembled, like a giant meccano set, on the site. The foundations were laid, and on 1 July 1887 the tower began to rise. Two hundred and fifty men worked from dawn to dusk, swinging the girders into place and driving in the red-hot rivets. All went according to plan, and the people of Paris watched their tower grow with astonishing speed.

The workers stood on tiny wooden platforms. The rivets were heated in small portable stoves. The girders were lifted into position by two cranes each weighing 50 tonnes. They slowly crawled up a central column, which was continually extended above them.

November 1887

March 1888

August 1888

December 1888

March 1889

An important feature of the tower was its lifts. A tall building is useless if people cannot get to the top quickly. Installing these was a real challenge, on a structure with slanting legs and of such great height. The lifts were not designed by Eiffel. The most successful, in the north and south legs, were made by an American firm, Otis. They took visitors from the ground to the second level.

Double-decker Otis lifts carried 50 passengers and moved at a speed of 2.1 m per second.

By March 1889 the Eiffel Tower was complete. At 300.51 metres, it was the highest structure in the world, a record it held until the construction of the Chrysler Building in New York in 1930. It had cost $1.6 million, and only one life. On 15 May 1889 the tower was opened to the public. It was an instant success. It was only designed to stand for 20 years, but it is still there today, as popular as ever. To date it has attracted over 185 million visitors. It remains the symbol of Paris, and a monument to the skill and bravery of Eiffel and his team.

The sixteen huge columns of the tower were adjusted to a fraction of a millimetre by tiny hydraulic jacks built into their bases. Two men pumped to force water into the jack. A third man drove in an iron wedge to fix the column.

The third platform is 274 m high. On a clear day you can see for up to 72 km. Above it is a small flat used by Eiffel.

The tower is built of wrought iron, held together by 2.5 million rivets. It weighs 8000 tonnes.

There was one lift in each of the four legs, taking visitors to the first and second platforms, and a fifth from the second platform to the top. All were operated by hydraulic power. The Otis lifts are shown in red.

The second platform is 115 m high. In 1889 there was a printing press and newspaper office there, as well as a bar and pastry shop.

The first platform is 57 m high. In 1889 there were four restaurants there, each serving a different style of food.

The four legs rest on massive concrete and stone blocks. Eiffel used caissons, like those used on the Brooklyn Bridge, to dig the foundations, as they were below the level of the River Seine.

The arches do not help in supporting the tower. Eiffel added them purely for decoration.

PANAMA CANAL

Engineers have done many wonderful things, but splitting a continent and joining two oceans must be one of the most spectacular. The Panama Canal, linking the Atlantic and Pacific oceans, is still probably the greatest single work of civil engineering in the world – construction on a gigantic, heroic scale.

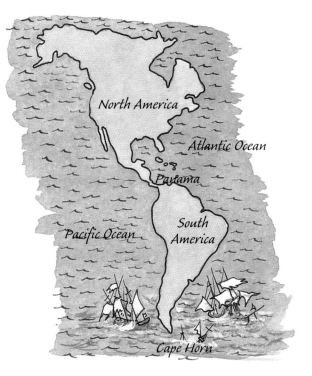

To sail from the Atlantic to the Pacific used to involve a very long and dangerous voyage of 19,000 kilometres, including the passage round Cape Horn at the tip of South America. Here, fierce winds and terrifying waves wrecked hundreds of ships. Both time and lives would be saved if a shorter route could be found. The obvious solution was to build a canal across the narrow strip of land joining North to South America. Digging a canal here had been suggested by a Spaniard as early as 1529, only 10 years after the 'discovery' of the Pacific by the explorer, Vasco de Balboa. But this just was not possible in those days.

Not everyone thought a canal was necessary. One plan proposed hauling ships from ocean to ocean on a giant railway.

Three hundred and fifty years later, in 1882, the first attempt to dig a canal was begun. The idea was that of a Frenchman, Ferdinand de Lesseps. He had built the Suez Canal in Egypt, which linked the Red Sea and the Mediterranean. Gustave Eiffel, another brilliant French engineer, was hired to design part of the canal, but after eight years of work in America, de Lesseps gave up. The fever-infested jungles had beaten him. Thousands of lives and millions of dollars had been lost.

The United States was very keen that the canal should be built, so that its Navy could move quickly between the east and west coasts. In 1903 the US bought a 16-kilometre wide strip of land in Panama, including the unfinished canal. Before any construction work could begin, the danger of disease had to be tackled. Yellow fever and malaria had killed 20,000 of de

Dr William C. Gorgas

Lesseps' workers. The scientific skill of Dr William C. Gorgas was vitally important here. He found that the diseases were spread by mosquitoes and, by draining swamps and spraying stagnant water with oil, he nearly exterminated them. Many workers still died, but not enough to stop the construction work.

Channels through the Gatun Lake and at the entrances were dug by huge dredgers. The endless chain of buckets was powered by steam engines. It could remove thousands of tonnes of mud each day.

The man in charge of construction was Colonel George W. Goethals of the US Engineers Corps.

Finally, work began. The machinery used was the largest and most modern of the time. Over 100 huge steam shovels, 553 mechanical drills, 50 cranes, 17 dredgers and a whole railway system with 160 locomotives and 4,500 trucks moved mountains of earth and rock.

Most of the digging was done by powerful steam shovels like these. The bucket could hold 4 m³ – the equivalent of a large skip. Each steam shovel did the work of 500 men with spades.

The canal was in three sections. More than half of its length was along a lake made by damming the Chiagres River. This lake was 26 metres above sea level, so three sets of locks were built to lift ships up and down. Each lock was big enough to raise a battleship by over 10 metres. The work of building these was stupendous. They were the largest structures in the world at the time, their walls and floors made entirely of reinforced concrete. Over 3.4 million cubic metres were poured, enough to make one Great Pyramid of Egypt, and a smaller one too.

The final section of the canal was a deep cutting through a mountain. There was no choice but to dig straight through. Four hundred million tons of rock and earth were moved. The rock was first broken up by explosives pushed into deep, drilled holes, and then dug out by steam shovel. Every day 10 tonnes of dynamite was exploded. The result was the Gaillard Cut.

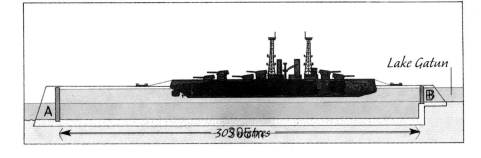

Lake Gatun

A

303 metres

B

The ship enters the lock through gate A. Water floods into the lock until the water level is the same as in Lake Gatun. Then gate B opens and the ship moves out, pulled by electric locomotives.

There were 46 gates in the three sets of locks. Each gate was made of steel plates riveted to a frame of steel girders. The largest gates were 25 m high and weighed 745 tonnes, as much as a small ship. The gates and valves to fill and empty the locks were moved by 1500 electric motors. This was the first time that such a huge engineering system relied on electric power alone.

Thousands of tourists came to see the canal works. A graduate from Harvard was hired to show them round and explain things.

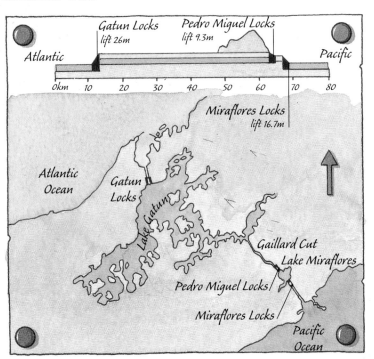

Gatun Locks
lift 26m

Pedro Miguel Locks
lift 9.3m

Atlantic

Pacific

0km 10 20 30 40 50 60 70 80

Miraflores Locks
lift 16.7m

Atlantic Ocean

Gatun Locks

Lake Gatun

Gaillard Cut
Lake Miraflores

Pedro Miguel Locks

Miraflores Locks

Pacific Ocean

In 1914, after 10 years of work and at a cost of nearly $400 million, the canal was finally opened to ships. The voyage from New York to San Francisco was immediately shorter by 12,700 kilometres.

WOOLWORTH BUILDING

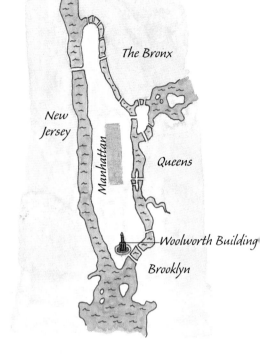

For hundreds of years only the towers of temples, churches and castles loomed over the cities of the world. It was not until the end of the 19th century that people began to build very tall buildings in which to live and work. Today, the skyscraper is as much the symbol of the modern world as the cathedral spire was the symbol of the medieval one.

The Tribune Building, New York.

The development that made skyscrapers possible was the use of iron and steel in building. What made them necessary was the growing population of cities during the 19th century, which made every single square metre of ground valuable. The use of an iron (later steel) frame for support meant buildings could be stronger and lighter, with thin walls. The Crystal Palace, built in London in 1851, showed it was possible to make a building of nothing but glass and iron. The Eiffel Tower showed that great heights could be reached safely.

In 1875 the tallest occupied building in the world was the Tribune Building in New York. It was 80 metres tall. New York City was the ideal place for skyscrapers. Manhattan was a small, crowded island. The city could only grow upwards. It was also made of rock, a good firm foundation for buildings. The first of the truly great New York skyscrapers was the Singer Building, built in 1907 to house the head office of the sewing machine company. It was 186 metres tall, with 47 storeys. The race was on to build even taller.

small windows

brick walls

In a normal brick building the walls bear all the weight. The taller the building, the thicker the walls at the bottom. This adds to the cost, and reduces the amount of space inside.

foundations

large windows

steel frame

An iron or steel-framed building is strong and light. The walls can be thin, as they don't do any of the work in holding up the building. Windows can be as large as they are wanted.

foundation pillars

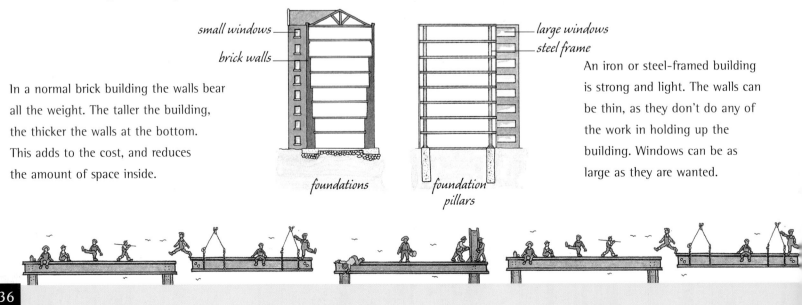

The most dangerous work was putting up the steel frame that weighed 45,000 tonnes, as much as an ocean liner. Men worked 200 m up in the air, running along steel beams only a few centimetres thick.

In 1909 Frank W. Woolworth decided to build the headquarters of his stores company on the best site in Manhattan, on Broadway. He hired a famous architect, called Cass Gilbert, who persuaded Woolworth to let him make this the tallest building in the world. Woolworth had travelled in Europe, where he had seen the great Gothic cathedrals. He wanted his new building to be in the neo-Gothic style. So Gilbert designed a skyscraper with carved arches, gargoyles in the shape of bats, flying buttresses, and a pyramid roof with intricate pinnacles and four turrets.

The main entrance leads to a lobby three storeys high. The outside has superbly detailed Gothic decoration, worthy of a medieval cathedral or palace.

A bronze sculpture inside the richly decorated entrance lobby shows Cass Gilbert with a model of the building.

As the streets of the business district of New York became lined with very tall buildings, the sun hardly ever reached the pavement. The City Council made a law that all skyscrapers over a certain height should be stepped back, so the full height was not directly over the street. This would allow more light to penetrate.

The tower was begun in August 1911 and finished in April 1913, at a cost of $13.5 million. It grew at the amazing rate of one and a half storeys a week. The outer skin was made of white stone and terracotta tiles, but inside was a steel skeleton. Its 60 storeys rose to a height of 241.5 metres, the tallest in the world at that time. The building held this record for 17 years, until it was topped by 40 Wall Street, New York.

The opening of the Woolworth building was a spectacular occasion. President Wilson sat in his office in Washington, 350 kilometres away, pressed a button – and 5000 windows in the great tower suddenly blazed with light.

Today the building is more like a small town than an office block. Fifteen thousand people work there, in shops and restaurants as well as offices.

CHEK LAP KOK AIRPORT

When aeroplanes first flew in the early 1900s they were so small and light they could land almost anywhere. Nobody imagined then that airports would become some of the largest, most complicated and most expensive structures on earth.

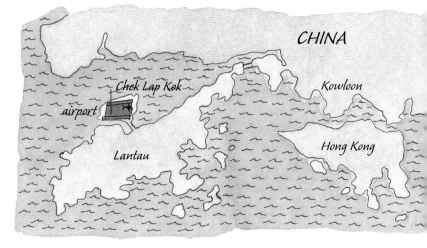

After the Second World War, commercial flying really took off. Planes became bigger and the number of passengers increased every year. Today, an airliner takes off somewhere in the world every three seconds. Airports have had to change to cope with these demands. Concrete runways have become longer and stronger, to take heavier planes, and the terminal buildings have grown in size and complexity.

The greatest airport yet built is Chek Lap Kok in Hong Kong, which opened in 1998. It was the largest construction project of the 1990s, and was voted one of the top ten buildings of the 20th century. The immense Y-shaped terminal building is the largest public space under one roof in the world, covering an area the size of a small town – it can even be seen from space. In the baggage hall, five jumbo jets could stand wing tip to wing tip.

London's first purpose-built modern airport was opened at Croydon in 1928. It was typical of airports in the 1930s and 40s. There was a terminal building, control tower and radio mast, offices and hangars for the planes. There were no hard runways. The planes landed on the grass field. All the buildings of the Croydon Airport could easily fit inside the terminal of Chek Lap Kok.

An army of earth-moving equipment was assembled to remodel the island. Dozens of excavators, bulldozers, scrapers, graders and dump trucks moved thousands of tons of soil and rock.

Building this incredible structure was a massive enterprise. The small mountain island of Chek Lap Kok, in Hong Kong harbour, had to be flattened and, at the same time, made four times larger. This was a major engineering project in itself, before any building work could begin. The work of quarrying and blasting went on 24 hours a day for two and a half years, and three quarters of the world's fleet of dredgers was involved in scooping up material to extend the island. It was joined to the mainland by a causeway, on which was built a railway line and a six-lane motorway.

The architect of the airport was Norman Foster, but the project was so enormous that no one man could possibly have designed it all. Foster led a huge team of architects and specialist engineers. The modern architect of a vast project is like the conductor of an orchestra, who makes sure that all the individual players come together at the right time to create a masterpiece.

The huge steel vaults of the airport roof were put together on the building site. 107,000 individual pieces of steel, made exactly to size in Singapore and the UK, were welded together by 700 workers to make the curved modules. These were then lowered into place by a crane capable of lifting 500 tonnes.

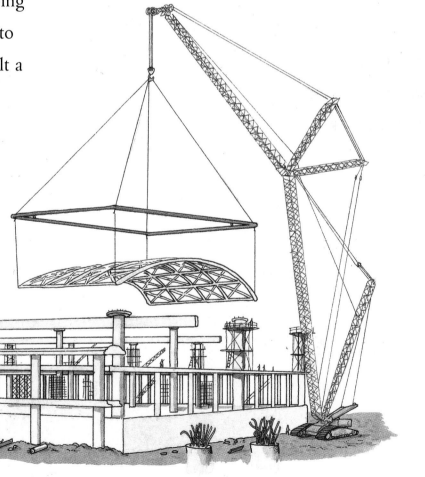

The roof of the terminal building is a vast assembly of steel vaults. They are made of steel shells, built in factories all over the world and assembled on site. The geometry of the curves is so complicated that it would have been impossible to design without computers. Foster wanted to design a building that, though huge, was also friendly, with wide uncluttered spaces lit with soft, natural light. Enormous windows give wide views of the surrounding dramatic landscape. This calm environment takes the stress out of flying and gives a new thrill to air travel.

Fact File

Number of passengers per day, without stress and overcrowding: 240,000
Number of luggage trolleys: 8000
Number of check-in desks: 288
Number of departure gates: 48
Distance from end to end: 1.27 km
Number of people employed there: 45,000
Cost to build: c.\$20 billion

control tower

maintenance hangars

aircraft loading gates

Chek Lap Kok, completed at the end of the 20th century, is the result of all the experience of architects and engineers stretching back to the pyramids. But it is not the end. Architects and engineers will continue to create larger and more wonderful buildings. These may even become 'intelligent', repairing and adapting themselves with the aid of robots. But whatever happens in the future, one thing is certain: as long as there are people in the world, the Great Pyramid will continue to awe, amaze and astonish them.

southern runway

Plan of the terminal building

diagonal concourse

west hall

north concourse

central concourse

immigration check-in

south concourse

0   100   200   300   400   500 m

Outside the terminal are huge hangars for servicing aircraft, an air cargo terminal, multi-storey car parks, bus and rail stations. The planes take off and land on two runways, each 3.8 km long.

Plan of the airport

north runway

terminal building

maintenance centre

control tower

rail and bus station

south runway

cargo terminal

motorway
railway

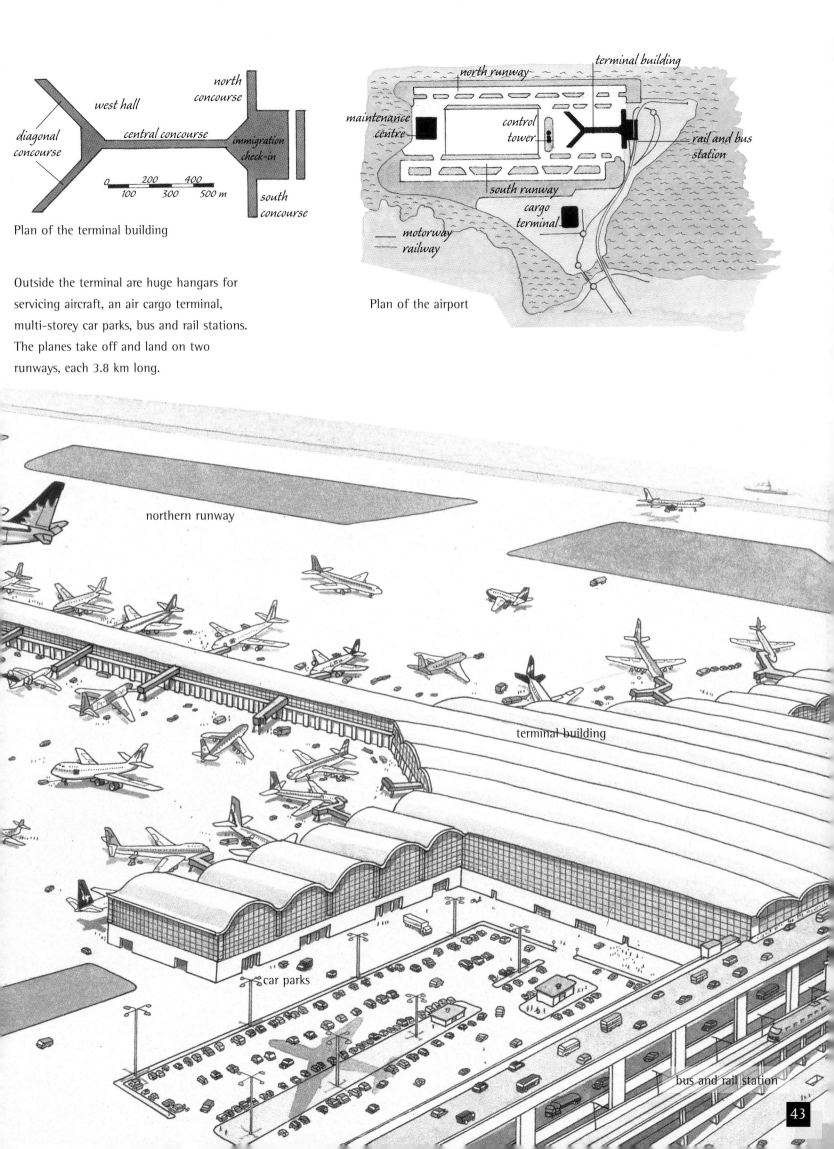

northern runway

terminal building

car parks

bus and rail station

GREAT BUILDINGS AROUND THE WORLD

The Parthenon, Athens, Greece is regarded by many as the most perfect building in the world. It was built by the ancient Greeks in 447 BC, as a temple to the goddess Athena. It is a simple structure, with no arches or domes. Its beauty lies in its subtle proportions and the wonderful statues that once decorated it. It was badly damaged by an explosion in 1687.

Sacsahuaman, Cuzco, Peru is a huge fortress, a spectacular example of Inca building. It was built 500 years ago. The walls are made from huge stone blocks, shaped to fit together so tightly that a knife cannot be pushed between them. All this was done with no mechanical aids and no iron tools.

Borobudur, Java is a great Buddhist temple pyramid. It was made by carving and building up a natural hill. It rises in eight terraces, lined with statues. It is the world's largest Buddhist shrine. Pyramids and mounds as sacred places are found all over the world.

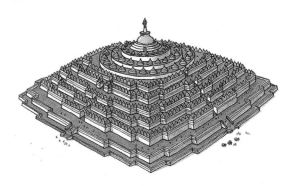

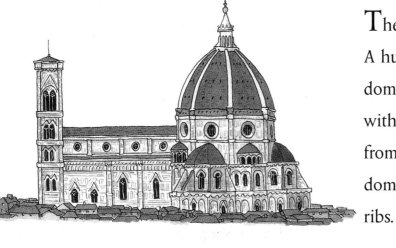

The cathedral, Florence, Italy was begun in 1296. A hundred years later it was finished, apart from the dome. No one knew how to build such a big dome without scaffolding to support it. The solution came from Renaissance architect Filippo Brunelleschi. His dome has two 'skins' of brick, supported on 24 stone ribs. It took 14 years to complete.

The Kariba Dam, Zambia was completed in 1959. It is 128 metres high, and its power station provides electricity for much of Zambia and Zimbabwe. Dams are some of the most spectacular creations of engineers. Since the 19th century they have been used to provide an artificial waterfall to drive electricity generators.

The Opera House, Sydney, Australia was designed by Danish architect Jørn Utzon. Engineer Ove Arup worked out a method to make Utzon's huge curving roofs stand up. The job of building the Opera House was so difficult it took fourteen years to finish - the building was finally opened in 1973.

The Øresund Bridge, Denmark and Sweden, is the central part of a new route, 16 kilometres long, that joins Denmark and Sweden. It is 7.5 kilometres long, with 64 spans, and carries a motorway and two rail tracks. It was opened in July 2000. Now for the first time trains and motor vehicles can travel from the north of Norway to the south of Spain without having to board a ferry.

INDEX